IN THEIR OWN WORDS

DAVY CROCKETT

George Sullivan

SCHOLASTIC REFERENCE

LIBRARY OF CONGRESS CATALOGING-IN-PUBLICATION DATA

Sullivan, George, 1927–
Davy Crockett/George Sullivan.
p. cm.—(In their own words)
Includes bibliographical references and index.
1. Crockett, Davy, 1786–1836—Juvenile literature. 2. Pioneers—Tennessee—Biography—Juvenile literature. 3. Frontier and pioneer life—Tennessee—Juvenile literature. 4. Tennessee—Biography—Juvenile literature. 5. Legislators—United States—Biography—Juvenile literature. 6. United States Congress House—Biography—Juvenile literature. 7. Alamo (San Antonio, Tex.) Siege, 1836—Juvenile literature. [1. Crockett, Davy, 1786–1836. 2. Pioneers. 3. Legislators.] I. Title. II. In their own words (Scholastic)
F436.C95 S85 2001
976.8'04'092—dc21
[B] 00-067032

ISBN 0-439-26318-2

12 11 6 7 8 9/0

Composition by Brad Walrod
Printed in the U.S.A. 40
First printing, October 2001

CONTENTS

CHAPTER 1

INTRODUCTION

"AS MY FATHER WAS VERY POOR, AND living as he did, far back in the back woods, he had neither the means nor the opportunity to give me or the rest of the children any learning.

"I stood no chance to become great in any other way than by accident."

These are the actual words of Davy Crockett. They are from his autobiography, the story of his life written by himself.

Davy's book was published in 1834. He was forty-eight years old.

Davy Crockett is a well-known figure in American history. Born in east Tennessee, he was a frontiersman and backwoods hunter. He was also a member of Congress. At one time during his career in politics, it was thought he might run for president. He fought for the independence of Texas.

Davy Crockett was tough and independent. He was proud, sensitive, and funny. He was also a great storyteller. These were skills that he used to win elections.

Through the years, much has been written about Davy Crockett. But a great deal of what has been written is not true. It is fiction.

Books called the Crockett almanacs portray him as a larger-than-life folk hero. These books became very popular in the years following Davy's death. And no wonder! They are rip-roaring adventure tales. They have colorful language and are full of surprises. They make people laugh.

These stories are like the fictional tales about Rip Van Winkle or Robin Hood. They are folklore. Nevertheless, many people believe all or parts of them to be true.

Television and movies discovered Davy Crockett in the 1950s and 1960s. Like the real Davy, the

Davy Crockett called this portrait by Samuel Stillman Osgood "the only correct likeness that has been made of me."

fictional one was depicted as a patriotic frontiersman, who was fair and kind. But like the Crockett almanacs, the TV shows and films contained little else that was factual.

Historians try to answer questions about people and the past. They use different kinds of sources for information. There are primary and secondary sources.

Primary sources are actual records that have been handed down from the past. Letters, diaries, and speeches are primary sources. Official government records and statistics are primary sources, too.

In the case of Davy Crockett, historians are lucky to have his autobiography as a primary source. It is titled *A Narrative of the Life of David Crockett of the State of Tennessee*. Davy wrote it during the winter of 1833–1834, with some help.

Davy was a poor speller. He said that correct spelling was "contrary to nature." He did not know English grammar well, either. Grammar, he said, was "nothing at all."

Davy, remember, was from the Tennessee

backwoods. Schools were rare there. Thomas Chilton, a friend and fellow member of Congress from Kentucky, helped Davy write his life story.

Letters written by Davy, his children, and grandchildren are also primary sources. So are copies of speeches that he made as a member of Congress.

Davy married twice. (His first wife died.) Historians use his marriage licenses as primary sources.

A secondary source is a description of an event by someone who did not witness the actual event. It is a secondhand source.

A history textbook is a secondary source. *The World Book* and other encyclopedias are secondary sources, too.

Historians use primary sources in helping to separate truth from fiction. For example, the Crockett almanacs describe Davy as being very tall and trim. One book says that he was "six-foot-four in his stocking feet."

But this is make-believe. Letters written by his grandchildren are more trustworthy. They say that

The Crockett almanacs said that Davy could "wade the Mississippi, carry a steamboat on his back, [and] whip his weight in wildcats."

Davy was of average height. He stood five-feet-seven or five-feet-eight. He had a muscular build.

The Crockett almanacs often show Davy in a coonskin cap. So do TV programs and movies about Davy. When hunting or living in the backwoods, Davy did wear rough clothes. Otherwise he wore a dark coat with a high collar that was in fashion at the time. He dressed in good taste.

"I don't think he ever had a picture made of him while in a hunting uniform," said Ashley Crockett, one of Davy's grandsons.

Pictures of Davy in a coonskin cap are "imaginary," he stated.

Primary sources help historians decide what is fact and what is fiction. They also can be exciting to read. In his life story, Davy takes the reader on a boat trip down the Mississippi. When Davy goes on a bear hunt, so does the reader. He tells how it feels to be very cold and hungry.

Davy Crockett was a man of independent spirit. He was a frontiersman and mighty hunter. As a member of Congress, he sought to help the poor.

It is little wonder that he is remembered as an American hero.

Still, the real story of Davy Crockett is often blotted out by legend. Primary sources can help to separate truth from fantasy. The story of Davy Crockett's life as he himself wrote it is a good example. It is, as Davy himself described it, "the exact image of the Author."

This book is a secondary source. But it makes use of primary sources, chiefly Davy Crockett's own life story. Its goal is the same as the life story itself—to present an "exact image" of Davy Crockett.

CHAPTER 2

BACKWOODS BOYHOOD

DAVY CROCKETT WAS BORN IN A simple log cabin in what is now east Tennessee. No records exist of his birth date. But August 17, 1786, is probably correct.

Davy would later write that he was born at the mouth of Limestone Creek on the Nolichucky River. A stone marker in Limestone, Tennessee, now identifies his birthplace.

Davy's parents, John and Rebecca Crockett, were pioneers. They helped to settle the wilderness beyond the frontier of the young United States. His father had been a soldier in the American Revolution. John was born either in Ireland or during his parents' voyage to

America. Davy's mother was from northern Maryland.

"My father and mother had six sons and three daughters," Davy recalled in his autobiography. "I was the fifth son."

When Davy was about seven, the family moved to another settlement. They stayed in eastern Tennessee, however, settling near the mouth of Cove Creek. There Davy's father and another man built a mill. Unfortunately, just as work on the mill was almost finished, a flood destroyed it.

"I remember the water rose so high," Davy said, "that it got up into the house we lived in, and my father moved us out to keep us from being drowned."

Afterward, the Crocketts moved again. They settled in Jefferson County, Tennessee, in 1794. There, on the road between Knoxville, Tennessee, and Abingdon, Virginia, the family opened a tavern. It was a place where travelers could rest and have something to eat.

One day when Davy was about twelve, a man

Davy Crockett's log cabin birthplace in Limestone, Tennessee.

named Jacob Siler stopped at the tavern. He was driving a herd of cattle to Rockbridge County in Virginia. The man told Davy's father that it was hard work. He needed help.

In those days, a young boy worked for his father. His father could also "hire out" his son to someone else. The boy would then turn over his pay to his father.

Davy's father hired him out to Mr. Siler. Davy had never been away from home. He didn't like the idea of leaving his family. He had no choice, however. He had been taught to obey. Still, as Davy later wrote, "I set out with a heavy heart."

On the cattle drive, Davy was a hard worker, but homesick. When they arrived in Rockbridge County, Mr. Siler was very kind to him. He wanted Davy to remain with him and not go back home.

Mr. Siler gave Davy several dollars. Davy understood what Mr. Siler was trying to do. "I think it was bait for me," Davy declared.

The money didn't matter to Davy. He longed for his family. He could think of nothing else. He waited for the chance to slip away from Mr. Siler.

One day Davy was playing with two other boys near Mr. Siler's home. Three wagons came down the road. They were being driven by an old man named Dunn and his two sons. Davy knew Mr. Dunn. He had often stayed at the Crockett tavern.

Davy told Mr. Dunn of his sad plight. He

explained that he wanted to get back to his mother and father. Would Mr. Dunn help him?

Mr. Dunn and his sons said they would. They made up a plan. "They told me," Davy recalled, "that they would stay at a tavern seven miles from there, and that if I could get to them before day the next morning, they would take me home."

That night before Davy went to bed, he gathered together all of his clothes and other belongings. He wrapped them in a tight bundle and put them under his bed. He wanted to be able to get away quickly the next morning.

Davy went to bed early that night. But he was so excited he could not sleep. "For though I was a wild boy," he wrote, "yet I dearly loved my mother and father, and . . . I could not sleep for thinking of them."

It was still pitch black when Davy left the Siler home. He found it was snowing hard outside. "The whole sky was hid by the falling snow," he remembered, "so I had to guess my way to the big road, which was a half mile from the house."

Davy Crockett's earliest memories were of the Tennessee backwoods and the Nolichucky River, pictured here.

By the time Davy reached the road, the snow was knee deep. But he realized that the snow was a blessing. It was falling so heavily that it covered his tracks. There would be no trail for Mr. Siler to follow.

It was still dark when Davy reached the tavern where the Dunns were staying. "Mr. Dunn took me in and treated me with great kindness," Davy recalled. "I warmed myself by the fire, for I was very cold..." After an early breakfast, they set out on their journey.

Davy could think of nothing but home. The wagons moved slowly through the drifting snow. Davy grew impatient. He knew that he could travel twice as fast walking.

The next morning Davy announced that he planned to set out on foot. The Dunns tried to stop him, but they could not persuade him to remain with the wagons.

Plodding through the deep snow, Davy was soon dead tired. Luckily, a man on horseback overtook him. The man was leading another horse. He offered to let Davy ride him.

"I traveled with him in this way..." Davy wrote, "until we got within fifteen miles of my father's house. There we parted, and he went on his way to Kentucky and I trudged on homeward, which place I reached that evening."

Later, when he was writing his life story, Davy was

unable to remember the name of the man who had helped him. "The name of this gentleman I have entirely forgotten," he wrote, "and I am sorry for it, for it deserves a high place in my little book." But his kindness, Davy said, "has . . . a resting place in my heart."

CHAPTER 3

RUNAWAY

IN THE FALL OF 1799, DAVY WAS JUST past his thirteenth birthday. His parents sent him to a small school that had opened near the Crockett home. Davy had never gone to school before. His brothers went with him.

On his fourth day of school, Davy quarreled with one of the older students. Davy knew the dispute could not be settled during school hours. The schoolmaster would punish them both for fighting.

Once the school day was over, Davy hid in the bushes and waited for the boy. When he passed by, Davy, as he put it, "set on him like a wild cat." He gave the boy a sound beating.

The next day, Davy was sure the schoolmaster

had heard about the fight. He would be waiting for Davy, ready to give him a thrashing.

Instead of going to school, Davy "laid out in the woods all day." When school was over, Davy joined his brothers and went home with them. He was able to persuade his brothers not to tell their father what he had done.

Davy continued to skip school for several days. Then the schoolmaster sent a note to Davy's father. He wanted to know why Davy wasn't in school.

When Davy arrived home later that day, his angry father was waiting for him. He wanted to know why Davy hadn't been going to school. Davy said that he was afraid to go, explaining that the schoolmaster was going to whip him.

Davy's father had no pity for his son. He seized a hickory stick and started after Davy, who raced from the house. His father chased him. Beyond the crest of a hill, Davy hid himself in roadside brush. His father ran by and didn't see him.

Davy spent the night at the home of Jesse Cheek, who lived a few miles from the Crocketts. Mr.

Cheek was about to start driving a herd of cattle to Front Royal, Virginia.

"I hired myself to go with him," Davy later recalled, "determining not to return home, as home and the schoolhouse had become too hot for me." An older brother decided he would go along with Davy.

Davy was gone from home for more than two years. He did more than drive cattle during that time. He also farmed and helped on wagon trains. In addition, he spent eighteen months working for a man who made and sold hats. When the hatter's business failed, the man fled the country. Davy, without any money, then made up his mind to return home.

He eventually made his way to the home of his uncle Joseph Crockett, one of his father's brothers. Davy was thrilled to find one of his own brothers there. It was the same brother who had left home with him more than two years before.

The two boys spent several weeks at their Uncle Joe's, and then they set out for home. Their journey ended late one evening in the spring of 1802. As the boys neared the family tavern, they noticed that several wagons had been left outside for the night. Davy knew the house would be crowded with wagon drivers and other guests.

Davy was now sixteen. His appearance had changed. He had grown several inches taller. A light stubble of beard covered his chin. He decided he would not announce his arrival. Instead, he would see whether anyone would be able to recognize him.

During the early evening, Davy did nothing to attract attention to himself. He hardly spoke to anyone.

"I had been gone so long, and had grown so much, that the family did not at first know me," Davy later recalled. "And another, and perhaps a stronger reason was, they had no thought or expectation of me, for they all had given me up as finally lost."

The guests were called to supper. After they had begun to eat, Davy's oldest sister began to look at him curiously. Suddenly she sprang up, dashed over

Long before he reached his teens, Davy was a crack shot. In the Crockett almanacs and elsewhere, he was often pictured with his favorite rifle.

to where Davy was sitting, and hugged him around the neck. "Here is my lost brother!" she cried out.

A tearful reunion followed. The family's joy made Davy feel ashamed that he had stayed away so long. He realized that he had caused the family great pain. He was sorry for what he had done.

Davy had not been home for very long when his father asked him for his help. Davy's father owed a farmer named Abraham Wilson thirty-six dollars, a large amount for the time. The debt was a great worry for Davy's father. He asked Davy whether he would go to work for Mr. Wilson until the debt was paid. Davy agreed to do so.

"I worked with all my might," Davy wrote, "not losing a single day in six months." Finally, the debt was paid.

Afterward, Davy went to work for John Kennedy, a Quaker from North Carolina. One day Mr. Kennedy told Davy that Davy's father owed him forty dollars. He said that if Davy would work for him for six months he would consider the debt to be paid.

Davy agreed to accept Mr. Kennedy's offer. "I concluded," Davy said, "that it was my duty as a child to help him along."

When Davy finished his six months of work, Mr. Kennedy gave him a statement saying the debt had been paid. One night at his parents' home, Davy gave the statement to his father.

Davy's father was deeply moved by what his son had done. Tears streamed down his cheeks. Davy wrote, my father said "he was sorry he couldn't give me anything, but he was not able, he was too poor."

In the weeks that followed, Davy continued to work for Mr. Kennedy. With the money he earned, he was able to buy himself clothes, a horse, and a rifle.

One day a young woman from North Carolina visited Mr. Kennedy's home. She was Mr. Kennedy's niece.

"I soon found myself head over heels in love with this girl," Davy wrote.

Davy had little experience in affairs of the heart. "When I would think of saying anything to her,"

Davy recollected, "my heart would begin to flutter like a duck in a puddle." The words he wanted to say got stuck in his throat.

Davy eventually managed to have a conversation with the young girl. She was engaged to be married, she told him. The news crushed Davy. But he realized that he had to accept the situation.

The experience started Davy thinking. He knew that he had many faults. His lack of schooling was his greatest failing. Davy could not read a simple children's book. He could not even name the first letter of the alphabet. He decided it was time to improve himself.

John Kennedy's married son had a small school. Davy agreed to work for him two days a week. In exchange, he would receive four days of schooling each week.

The arrangement continued for six months. "In this time," said Davy, "I learned to read a little in my primer [and] write my own name." He also learned simple arithmetic.

After about 100 days of schooling, Davy quit. He had other things on his mind.

“I should have continued longer,” he admitted in his autobiography, “if it hadn’t been that I concluded I couldn’t do any longer without a wife, and so I cut out to hunt me one.”

CHAPTER 4

LOVE AND MARRIAGE

NOT LONG AFTER DAVY QUIT SCHOOL to seek a bride, he visited a family of what he called "very pretty girls." It was a family that he had known when he was younger.

One of the girls attracted him very much. Her name was Margaret Elder. "I got to love her as bad as I had the Quaker's niece," Davy declared. Margaret eventually agreed to marry Davy. The couple set a wedding date.

Not long before the marriage was to take place, Davy went off with his friends for a weekend of fun. He took his rifle. There was a shooting contest, which Davy won. There was dancing and partying.

When the festivities ended, Davy traveled to Dandridge, Tennessee, where Margaret lived. On the way he visited the county courthouse to get their marriage license. According to court records, he received the license on October 21, 1805. Davy was nineteen.

Meanwhile, word of Davy's weekend of merriment reached Margaret's ears. She didn't like what she heard. The news caused her to change her mind about Davy.

Before Davy reached Margaret's home, he stopped at the home of her uncle for a friendly visit.

Margaret's sister happened to be there. Davy asked her about Margaret. The girl gave Davy a troubled look. Suddenly she burst into tears. She then spilled out startling news. Her sister was no longer interested in Davy. In fact, she was planning to marry another man the very next day.

Davy, as he wrote, was struck "perfectly speechless." He felt so weak he thought he was going to fall to the floor.

Margaret's sister felt sorry for Davy. She urged him

to visit Margaret and try to change her mind. Her parents, she told him, preferred Davy to the man Margaret was about to wed.

Davy had no wish to see Margaret. He accepted his fate. "I bid her farewell," Davy remembered, "and turned my lonesome and miserable steps back again homeward, concluding that I was only born for hardships, misery, and disappointment."

Davy's distress did not last very long. Several months later, he attended a party. "An old Irish woman . . . came up to me," he wrote, "and began to praise my red cheeks and said she had a sweetheart for me."

The sweetheart was the woman's daughter. Her name was Mary Finley. She was nicknamed Polly.

Davy soon learned that Polly had another suitor. She preferred Davy, though. Three months after their first meeting, they agreed to marry.

On August 12, 1806, five days before his twentieth birthday, Davy got a second marriage license. This time a wedding followed. The couple rented a small cabin near Elk River, Tennessee. Davy farmed the land and hunted.

Davy enjoyed hunting on the game-rich land of Elk River, Tennessee.

Three children were born to the Crocketts. They were named John Wesley, William, and Margaret.

Life was not easy for the young couple and their children. After a time, Davy felt a change was in order.

"We worked for some years, renting ground, and paying high rent," he stated, "until I found it wasn't the thing it was cracked up to be, and I couldn't make a fortune at it . . . So I concluded to quit it, and set out for some new country."

The Crocketts packed their belongings onto two horses. Traveling west, they crossed the mountains into Lincoln County, Tennessee. It was the first in a series of moves that would take the family across the length of the state.

Lincoln County offered rich land and plenty of game. "It was there," as Davy put it, "that I began to distinguish myself as a hunter and to lay the foundation for all my future greatness."

CHAPTER 5

THE CREEK WAR

THE FRONTIER KEPT MOVING WESTWARD. The backwoods country was once heavily wooded and unsettled. Bit by bit the land became dotted with farms and small villages. Restless settlers pushed the frontier back through Kentucky and Tennessee.

As the frontier moved, Davy and his family moved with it. Early in 1813, the Crocketts headed farther west to Franklin County, Tennessee. They settled down in a log cabin home on Bean's Creek about ten miles south of the town of Winchester. Tennessee's southern border with Alabama was not far away.

The frontier was not empty. Native Americans

lived there. They often guided the new settlers, leading them to food and water.

Several Native American nations occupied Tennessee and the land that was to become the southeastern United States. The Creek nation was the most powerful one. Creek warriors were known for their bravery.

In time, bad feelings developed between the Creeks and the white settlers. The Creeks said that the settlers had broken treaties with them. Now the settlers were living illegally on Creek land.

During the summer of 1813, while Davy and his family were living in Franklin County, war broke out between the Creeks and the settlers. The settlers struck first. The assault took place at Burnt Corn Creek in what is now Alabama. A force of almost 200 soldiers opened fire upon a band of Creek warriors as they rested. Many Creeks died.

The settlers knew that the Creeks would seek revenge—and they did. Hundreds of Creek warriors attacked Fort Mims on the lower Alabama River. Careless guards had failed to close the fort's gate. The

Creeks poured through to slaughter those inside. Some 500 soldiers and settlers died. The Creeks also suffered heavy losses.

The settlers were shocked and horrified. A call went out for volunteers to fight the Creeks. From these volunteers, a militia unit would be formed.

Davy signed up, even though Polly begged him not to do so. She said she didn't want to be left alone in the wilderness to raise their young children.

Davy had made up his mind to fight. He could not be swayed. "I reasoned the case with her as well as I could," Davy wrote, "and told her, that if every man would wait till his wife got willing for him to go to war, there would be no fighting done, until we would all be killed in our own houses . . ."

General Andrew Jackson led the Tennesseans during the Creek War. The forty-six-year-old Jackson was an important figure in Tennessee politics. He had been elected to Congress in 1796, the same year that Tennessee had entered the union. Jackson won a seat in the United States Senate in 1797.

General Andrew Jackson commanded army forces in the Creek War. In 1829, he became the seventh U.S. president.

Davy became a scout under General Jackson's command. Because of his skill and experience as a backwoodsman, Davy was chosen to lead a company of troops into Creek country. He and his men returned with urgent news. A Creek war party was on its way to attack General Jackson and his troops.

The colonel to whom Davy reported paid no attention to the important news. The next day, one of the colonel's officers returned with a report that was the same as Davy's. The Creeks were coming! This time the colonel flew into action, ordering defenses to be built.

The incident made Davy bitter. He believed the colonel had not listened to him because he was not of high rank. He wrote, "When I made my report, it wasn't believed, because I was no officer... just a poor soldier. But when the officer reported the same thing, it was all as true as preaching."

Once during his tour of duty, Davy sat in on a meeting with General Jackson and an army captain. The discussion concerned a young soldier who would not obey one of the captain's orders. General Jackson quickly settled the matter in the captain's favor.

Davy was later asked what General Jackson had said. Davy summed up the general's words by saying, "The old general told the captain to be sure he was right and then go ahead."

The saying soon became popular within the army. It later spread far and wide.

The phrase became Davy's motto. He became known as the "Go Ahead" man. He would sometimes sign letters or photos, "Be always sure you're right, then go ahead."

Early in November 1813, Davy and the troops of his regiment marched from Tennessee into Alabama. Near the town of Gadsden, they took part in the battle of Tallussahatchee. It was a tragic defeat for the Creeks. "The enemy fought with savage fury," General Jackson later wrote, "and met death with all its horrors."

Not long before Christmas Day in 1813, Davy's term of enlistment ended. He returned home to his wife and children. Davy was at home less than a year. In the fall of 1814, another call for troops went out. Davy signed up a second time.

This time Davy was assigned to scout for Creeks in the swamps of Florida. Food was in short supply. At times, Davy and the other soldiers were on the brink of starvation. His sharpshooting skills were put to important use. Davy spent most of his time hunting wild game for food.

Davy went home before the final stages of the war. He paid a young man to serve in his place until his tour of duty ended. Soldiers were allowed to do that at the time.

Davy was not present when General Jackson scored an important victory over the Creeks at the Battle of Horseshoe Bend in central Alabama. The battle helped to bring the Creek War to a close. The Treaty of Fort Jackson was signed on August 9, 1814. The Creeks were made to give up two-thirds of their land.

After the defeat of the Creeks at the battle of Horseshoe Bend, Creek leader Red Eagle surrendered to General Jackson, ending the Creek War.

Back home, Davy had to face what he called "the hardest trial which ever falls to the lot of man." In the fall of 1815, Davy's wife, Polly, became ill and died. He buried her near their home.

Davy was left with three small children to raise. One of them was an infant daughter.

Davy got his brother and his wife to move in with him to help care for the children. The arrangement didn't work out, however. "I came to the conclusion it wouldn't do," Davy stated, "but that I must have another wife."

CHAPTER 6

A PLUNGE INTO POLITICS

A WIDOW WITH TWO CHILDREN LIVED not far from Davy's home. Her name was Elizabeth Patton. Her husband had been killed in the Creek War.

"She was a good industrious woman," Davy said, "and owned a snug little farm, and lived quite comfortable."

Davy began calling on Elizabeth. She enjoyed his visits. As Davy put it, "My company was not at all disagreeable to her."

Davy and Elizabeth were married in 1816. They had three children. They named them Robert, Rebecca, and Matilda.

Elizabeth was a woman with good sense. She

was skilled in managing a household. Within a year or so of their marriage, Davy's fortunes began to rise.

In 1817, the Crocketts moved about eighty miles west to what would become Lawrence County, Tennessee. There Davy built a log cabin near the mouth of Shoal Creek. Their nearest neighbor was seven miles away.

Lawrence County was raw frontier land. There was no government. There was no law. The new settlers met and set up a temporary government. They asked Davy to be a judge.

Davy had never studied law. He admitted that he could barely write his own name. As he had before, he worked hard. He quickly learned to keep court records and prepare legal papers.

The people of Lawrence County came to trust in Davy's fairness. "I gave my decisions on the principles of common justice and honesty between man and man," recollected Davy, "and relied on natural born sense, and not on law, to guide me."

Davy became a popular person in Lawrence County. In 1818, he was named the commissioner

For a frontier family, life had its difficult moments. Here Davy's wife helps him to subdue a great black bear. This illustration is from one of the Crockett almanacs.

for the new town of Lawrenceburg. About the same time, he was elected to the rank of colonel in the local militia.

Davy thought it might be a good idea to give politics a try. In 1821, he sought election as a member of the Tennessee legislature, the state's law-making body. Davy had no experience as a candidate for public office. He was terrified at the thought of having to make a speech. He said, "I choaked [choked] up as bad as if my mouth had been jamm'd and cramm'd chock full of dry mush."

Davy developed his own strategy. He would let the "big candidates," as he called them, speak all day. "When they quit," Davy noted, "the people were worn out with fatigue."

Then it was Davy's turn to speak. He knew he had a gift for entertaining people. "I got up and told some laughable story," he wrote.

The voters liked Davy's humorous speaking style. He won the election.

Not long after his victory, Davy met James K. Polk. Polk was also a member of the state legislature.

After they were introduced, Polk spoke to Crockett. "Well, Colonel," he said, "I suppose we shall have a radical change of the judiciary at the next session of the legislature."

Davy's brow wrinkled. He didn't know what the word *judiciary* meant. He didn't know that it referred to judges and the law courts.

He was quick to answer, though. "Very likely, Sir," Davy replied.

Afterward, Davy was afraid someone was going to ask him what the judiciary was. "I don't indeed

James K. Polk served with Davy in the Tennessee state legislature. Polk was later a U.S. Congressperson and the governor of Tennessee. In 1845, Polk became the eleventh U.S. president.

believe I had ever before heard that there was such a thing in all nature," he later recalled.

By the time the state legislature held its first meeting, Davy made sure he knew what the judiciary was. "And what the government was, too," he said, "and many other things I had known nothing about before."

In 1822, the Crocketts moved again. Davy had

found land that he liked about 150 miles to the north and west, not far from the Obion River.

It was wild country. It was thick with deer, bear, and other kinds of game. Many Native Americans lived there.

John Wesley, Davy's oldest son, and another young man helped Davy build a log cabin on the site. They cleared the land and planted corn. They hunted for food. One of the bears they killed weighed 600 pounds.

After Davy butchered the animals, he salted the meat. It could then be stored for future use.

The animal skins were valuable, too. Davy sold them. With the money he received, Davy bought other foods his family needed. These included salt, sugar, flour, and coffee.

In 1823, Davy ran a second time for a seat in the state legislature. One of his opponents was Dr. William Butler. He was a well-educated man of some wealth.

In his campaign, Davy made it clear that he would continue to work hard for the men and women of

While campaigning, Davy, like other candidates for public office, often addressed voters from atop a tree stump.

west Tennessee. At the same time, he painted Dr. Butler as a man who lived in great luxury.

One day, Davy happened to be campaigning in Dr. Butler's hometown. Being a friendly person, Dr. Butler invited Davy to his home for dinner.

When Davy stepped inside the home, he was dazzled by the elegant furniture and decorations. One rug, in particular, caught his eye. Soft and thick, it was the most expensive rug he had ever seen. In Davy's log cabin home, the floors were covered with bearskins.

During the evening, Davy would not let his feet touch Dr. Butler's lovely rug. He was careful to walk around it.

Back on the campaign trail, Davy used Dr. Butler's fine rug as an example. He wanted to point out the difference between Dr. Butler's wealthy lifestyle and the way most Tennesseans lived. Davy told the crowds that Dr. Butler walked on fabric that was "finer than any gowns your wife or your daughters, in all their lives, ever *wore*."

In the election, Davy defeated Dr. Butler and the other opponents. He went back to the state legislature for a second term.

Davy continued to be devoted to the people of west Tennessee and their lands. He introduced bills to provide for land surveys. He supported laws to protect the people from land swindlers. Improving the navigation of rivers was another of Davy's concerns.

Davy's popularity kept building. He was becoming known from one end of Tennessee to the other.

One day as his second term in the state legislature was drawing to a close, friends of Davy's came to him with a plan. They wanted him to run for a seat in the U.S. House of Representatives in Washington, D.C.

At first, Davy said no. He felt he wasn't ready to serve as a representative. "It was a step above my knowledge," he said.

Davy's friends kept pressing him to run. Finally, he agreed to enter the race.

In the election later that year, Davy was defeated by a narrow margin. One reason for his loss was a lack of money. He simply couldn't afford to campaign through the entire state.

Davy now realized that popularity was not enough for success in politics. A candidate also needed money. Back home in the fall of 1825, making money became his goal.

C H A P T E R 7

CLOSE CALLS

DAVY HAD A PLAN FOR MAKING money. When he returned home in the fall of 1825, he put the plan into action.

The land near Davy's home was thickly forested with cypress trees. From cypress, Davy knew, barrel staves could be made. Staves are the long, narrow, curved pieces of wood used to form the sides of tubs and barrels.

Davy went into the barrel-stave business. He hired some workers to help him. They began chopping down the cypress trees. Then they cut the trunks into thin strips.

Davy had some of the men build two boats on the shore of the Obion River near his property. The Obion flowed west to join the Mississippi

River at a point about seventy miles north of Memphis.

Davy's plan was to load the barrel staves aboard the boats. He and his men would then float them down the Obion to the Mississippi, and then to New Orleans. Once there, Davy would sell the staves. He hoped to sell the boats, too.

Davy worked with the men for only a short time. Cutting down cypress trees bored him. Hunting was what he wanted to do. Besides, his family needed meat for the winter. Taking a rifle and several hunting dogs, Davy headed for the woods in search of bear.

It didn't take Davy long to kill the game his family needed. He had hardly returned home when one of his neighbors asked Davy to come and hunt on his land with him. Davy could not resist. He went hunting again. He and his neighbor killed fifteen bears on that trip.

When Davy returned, he went back to work with the men he had hired. The lure of hunting was again too great. He set out a third time. One of his sons went with him.

One day at dusk, Davy's dogs started barking loudly. They had picked up the scent of a bear. As they dashed off on the trail of the bear, Davy followed, his rifle in hand. Davy scrambled over fallen logs and struggled through thick undergrowth. The dogs chased the bear up a tall poplar tree.

When Davy reached the scene, he looked up into the tree. He could hardly make out the bear. In the dark, all he could see was a shapeless mass. Davy put his rifle to his shoulder. "I pointed as near the lump as I could," he later recalled, "and I fired away."

The bear climbed higher. Davy reloaded and fired again.

The bear tumbled to the ground, still alive. Davy fired a third time. The bear did not fall. There was no time to reload. Davy tossed his rifle aside and drew out his knife. With the bear about to charge, Davy lunged at the animal, killing it.

When Davy returned home, he found that his workers had made close to 30,000 barrel staves. The boats were almost finished and ready to be loaded.

In 1841, one of the Crockett almanacs presented an article titled "Tussel with a Bear" along with this cover illustration.

Early in February 1826, Davy got under way for New Orleans.

Davy took along several men to help him operate the boats. But they, like Davy, had no experience as sailors.

All went well at first. The boats made their way down the Obion River without any difficulty. When they reached the Mississippi, it was different.

Davy and his men were in awe of the size of the river. It was so wide it was almost like sailing on the ocean. The flow of the current ran much swifter than the Obion's. They found they had little control over their heavily loaded boats.

Davy had to come up with a quick plan. He told the men to lash the two boats together to make them easier to steer. Unfortunately, the idea didn't work. The boats went wherever the current carried them.

In the evening, Davy intended to pull into shore for the night. However, he and his men were unable to get the boats close enough to the riverbank to tie up.

Several times throughout the night, they tried to land but they couldn't. They could see people on the shore at the landing places. They ran about with lanterns and shouted directions to Davy and his crew. The boats continued to be swept along with the river's flow. "At last we quit trying to land," Davy recollected, "and concluded to go ahead as well as we could."

At some time during the night, Davy left the boat's upper deck and went below to warm himself. He thought about how much better it would be to be out bear hunting than floating along on the water. He felt like a piece of driftwood.

Suddenly, Davy heard the men on the deck above running about in great confusion. Then there was a loud crash, and Davy was sent sprawling.

The boats had struck floating tree trunks and other debris that had collected in the river near a small island. As the men watched helplessly, the boats veered around and began to float sideways. Then Davy's boat began to be sucked underwater, beneath the forward boat.

Davy, still below deck, had no idea what was happening. He tried to reach his men above. But water was pouring through the hatchway that led to the upper deck. He was trapped!

He saw one chance of escape. In the room in which Davy found himself, a small hole had been cut in the side of the boat. Its purpose was to allow people below deck to scoop water out of the river.

Davy studied the hole. It seemed too small for him to get through. It was his only chance, though. He stuck his arms and head through the hole. Then he started yelling as loud as he could.

The men on the other boat heard him. They reached down and grabbed Davy's arms and started pulling. His body hardly budged. His boat was taking on more and more water.

"I told them," Davy later wrote, "to pull my arms off, [to] force me through."

The men pulled harder. Davy's body started moving. He felt his clothes being ripped from his body. He felt his skin being torn away.

By pulling and jerking, the men finally dragged

Davy through the opening. He was alive, but in great pain. "I was literally skin'd like a rabbit," as he put it.

Davy lay almost naked on the deck of the boat that rescued him. He watched sadly as the other boat slowly disappeared beneath the water's surface.

The rescue boat seemed about to sink, too. To save their lives, Davy and his men had to leave their boats and cargo. They jumped to the mass of logs that their boats had hit. There they spent the rest of the night. In the morning a small boat picked them up and brought them downriver to Memphis.

Davy and his crew were welcomed like heroes. Grateful to be alive, Davy entertained the crowd that greeted them with jokes and colorful stories.

By the late spring of 1826, Davy was back home. He never recovered his two boats or the thousands of barrel staves. As a result, he suffered a serious financial loss.

In the following year, 1827, Davy decided to run again for election to the U.S. House of Representatives. Together the Senate and the

House of Representatives form the U.S. Congress. Davy had to borrow $250 to pay his campaign expenses.

Davy traveled all over the state of Tennessee, speaking to voters. He pointed with pride to his record as a soldier in the Creek War and as a member of the state legislature. His humorous stories amused audiences. This time, Davy won the election to the U.S. Congress by a wide margin.

Late in the fall of 1827, Davy set out from his home on horseback. He traveled across rivers and mountains. He made his way into east Tennessee and then Virginia. On December 27, 1827, he arrived in the nation's capital, Washington, D.C. Davy Crockett was ready to begin his career in national politics.

CHAPTER 8

IN CONGRESS

THE NEW CONGRESS MET FOR THE first time on December 3, 1827. From the beginning, Davy's chief concern was the people of the area of Tennessee that he represented and the land on which they lived.

The people of Davy's district had helped to push the American frontier to the west. They were pioneers, like his parents. The land they had settled was rough and wild. Much of it was owned by the United States government. They were called squatters because they held no deed or title to the land on which they lived.

Davy sought to help the squatters. They had struggled to improve the land. They made their homes on it and raised their families there. Davy believed that they should be able to own it.

Davy wanted the federal government to turn over the land it owned to the state of Tennessee. Then the state could sell it cheaply to the poor.

"The rich require but little legislation," stated Davy. "We should at least occasionally legislate for the poor."

Congress kept putting off voting on Davy's proposal. Davy was disappointed. "There's too much talk [in Congress]," declared Davy. "Many men seem to be proud that they can say so much about nothing. Their tongues keep working, whether they've got any grist to grind or not."

Davy became very popular among the people of west Tennessee. They found him to be truthful and honest. His support of squatters' rights made them grateful.

Then, as now, each member of the House of Representatives served a two-year term. Davy ran for reelection in 1829. He won easily.

During Davy's first term in Congress, John

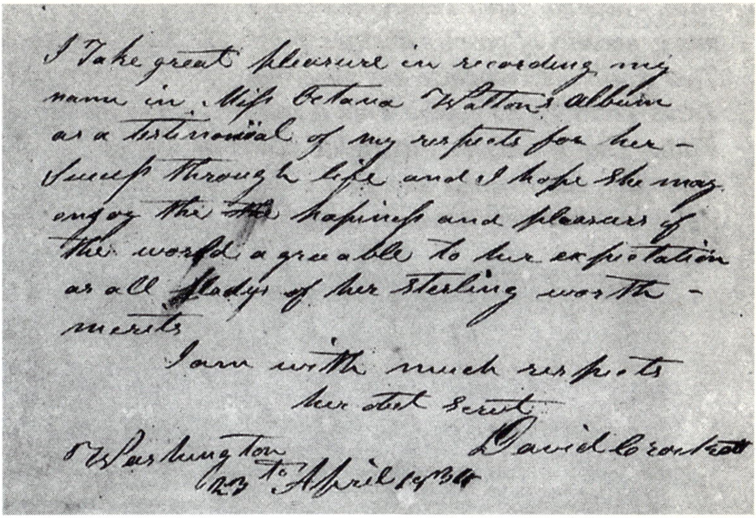

I Take great pleasure in recording my name in Miss Octavia Walton's album as a testimonial of my respects for her - Success through life and I hope she may enjoy the happiness and pleasures of this world agreeable to her expectation as all Ladys of her sterling worth - merits

I am with much respects
her obdt Servt
David Crockett

Washington
23rd April 1834

As a member of Congress, Davy was ever mindful of the people he represented. Not long after being elected in 1834, he wrote this note in response to a request for his autograph.

Quincy Adams had been president. When Adams sought reelection in 1828, he was defeated by Andrew Jackson.

Davy knew Jackson well, of course. He had been Davy's commanding officer in the Creek War.

The powerful Jackson expected total support from his followers. While Davy agreed with many of President Jackson's policies, he would not follow him blindly.

To show the voters how he felt about Jackson, Davy told a simple story: A boy worked for his master as a farmhand. One day the master told the boy to plow across one of the fields until he got to the red cow.

The boy began to plow. As he plowed, the cow started moving. The boy kept after her, plowing. The cow kept moving. The boy plowed all afternoon, following the cow wherever she went.

When the master returned, he shrieked in anger. The cow had wandered aimlessly over the master's field. Everywhere the cow had gone, the boy had trailed behind. The field was ruined.

Davy said that he would never be like the boy in the red-cow story. He would not follow the cow wherever it went.

"As long as General Jackson went straight, I followed him," Davy said. "But when he began to go this way, and that way, and every way, I wouldn't go after him."

Davy and President Jackson clashed over the

Indian Removal Act. The Act gave the federal government the power to seize the land of the Native Americans. Then they would have to move to new land west of the Mississippi River.

In the Southeast, five Native American nations were involved. They were the Creek, Cherokee, Choctaw, Chickasaw, and Seminole. Members of these nations lived mostly in Georgia, Alabama, and Mississippi.

Davy opposed the Indian Removal Act. It was not fair, he said. Native Americans had no voice in the matter. The Act was to be forced upon them. Davy called it a "wicked unjust measure."

Many of the people of west Tennessee didn't like Davy's stand. They were hungry for land that was good for farming. To the east, such land had already been purchased and was occupied.

That wasn't the only reason. By buying land cheap, then selling it, a backwoodsman could escape poverty. He might even end up with a sizeable amount of money for himself.

Those seeking control over land liked the idea of the Creeks being removed from their state. Once they were gone, the land on which the Creeks had lived would be made available to white settlers.

President Jackson supported the Indian Removal Act. He pushed hard to get it made into law.

On May 19, 1830, Congress voted on the Act. Davy voted against it. But Jackson controlled most

Like several other Native American tribes in the southeast United States, the Creeks were forced to give up their lands and move west. American artist and author George Catlin sketched these drawings of Creeks in 1834.

of the votes. The bill became law. Afterward, President Jackson was furious with Davy for opposing him.

When Davy returned home to Tennessee, he quickly saw that many people had turned against him. He had opposed Jackson and the Indian Removal Act. "I found the storm had raised against me sure enough," Davy said, "and it was echoed from side to side, and from end to end of my district, that I had turned against Jackson. This was considered the unpardonable sin."

Davy ran for reelection in 1831. Jackson's supporters worked hard to defeat him. They picked out his opponent, a lawyer and judge named William Fitzgerald.

They gave out handbills in support of Fitzgerald. They sent speakers into Davy's district to praise Fitzgerald and insult Davy.

Jackson's supporters also played a dirty trick or two. Without telling Davy, they would give out word that he was going to appear at a certain place at a particular time. A crowd would gather on the announced day to hear Davy speak. He didn't know about the gathering. Instead, a Fitzgerald supporter would be there to speak. He would tell the people that Davy was afraid to attend. In this way, Davy noted, "[they] would turn many against me."

The election was close, but Davy lost.

Davy was bitter. "I have not got a collar round my neck with the name Andrew Jackson on it," he declared. "Because I would not take the collar, I was hurled from the party."

After his defeat, Davy returned home. He hunted. He tended his farm. Davy knew that in two years another election would take place. He would be ready.

CHAPTER 9

TOURING THE NORTHEAST

DAVY RAN FOR CONGRESS AGAIN IN 1833. William Fitzgerald ran against him for a second time. This time Davy won.

Davy was becoming famous throughout the entire nation. For many Americans, he had come to represent the pioneering spirit of the frontier.

A play titled *The Lion of the West* had Eastern audiences cheering. Nimrod Wildfire, the play's leading character, was based upon Davy and his backwoods life.

Late in 1833, the play was performed at a Washington theater. A fine comic actor named James Hackett, who closely resembled Davy, played the role of Colonel Nimrod Wildfire.

One evening, Davy went to the theater to see the play. An overflow audience was on hand. When the theater manager led Davy to his seat, the crowd broke into applause and cheers.

When the cheering ceased, the house lights dimmed and the curtain rose. Onto the stage strode James Hackett. He wore a fringed hunting shirt, buckskin pants, and a fur cap. The actor took note of the applause and then turned toward Davy and bowed deeply.

Davy, fine looking in his best city suit, grinned. He then rose and bowed right back. The audience went wild.

A biography about Davy, titled *The Life and Adventures of Colonel David Crockett of West Tennessee*, was published in 1833. It was an instant success.

Davy then decided to write his own story of his life. He was humble about his lack of writing skills. He asked fellow congressperson Thomas Chilton of Kentucky to help write his book. In it, he told what life was like on the frontier. He recited colorful

In this engraving based on a portrait by Asher Brown Durand, Davy penned his motto: "I have this rule for others when I am dead, be always sure you are right, then go ahead."

hunting tales. The book was filled with Davy's humor and political opinions. It also repeated his motto—"Be always sure you're right, then go ahead."

Because of his growing popularity, Davy attracted the interest of the Whigs, a political party formed in 1834. The Whigs opposed President Jackson and his policies. Since Davy was the foremost of Jackson's enemies, the Whigs were attracted to him. They thought that Davy might make a good candidate for president.

The Whigs arranged for Davy to visit several big cities of the Northeast. The tour was meant to test support for Davy, should he make a run for the presidency. It was also to be used to promote sales of Davy's book.

Davy left Washington on April 25, 1834, for Baltimore, his first stop on the tour. He dined with Whig supporters that evening. The next morning he left for Philadelphia by steamboat.

When the vessel eased into its dock, a huge crowd was there to greet him. Davy was amazed. "I saw the whole face of the earth covered with people," Davy later recalled, "all looking anxiously toward the boat."

Davy was led to an elegant four-wheeled carriage

drawn by four horses. Davy described the scene: "The streets were crowded in a great distance, and the windows full of people, looking out I suppose to see the wild man. I thought I had rather be in the wilderness with my gun and dogs, than be attracting all that fuss."

Davy visited the sights in Philadelphia. His new Whig friends were with him every step of the way.

A group of young Whigs presented Davy with a fine rifle. Davy was thrilled with the gift. "I love a good gun," Davy said, "for it makes a man feel independent, and prepared for either war or peace."

In Philadelphia during his tour of the Northeast, Davy gave a rousing speech to an enthusiastic audience, as did Daniel Webster (above), U.S. senator from Massachusetts. Webster, like Davy, was an opponent of Andrew Jackson's.

Davy called his old

rifle "Betsey." He named his new one "Pretty Betsey." He promised to keep the gun "so long as I am in existence."

When Davy arrived in New York City, a group of Whigs was there to greet him. On the first evening of his visit, Davy was sitting with friends when he heard the cry of "Fire! Fire!" Davy leaped from his chair and bolted for the door.

"Sit down, Colonel!" said one of the men. "It's not near us."

"Ain't you going to help put it out?" Davy asked.

"No," the man said, laughing. "We have fire companies here and we leave it to them."

To Davy, this seemed odd. "At home," he later recalled, "I would have jumped on the first horse at hand, and rode full flight, bare-backed, to help put out the fire."

At City Hall, Davy met the mayor of New York. Davy found him to be "a plain, common-sense looking man."

Davy was also taken to Five Points, a crowded, run-down part of the city. "What a miserable place is a city for poor people," Davy noted. "They are all half-starved and poorly clothed." Davy wondered why "they do not clear out for a new country."

From New York, a steamer carried Davy and his party to Newport, Rhode Island. It was then on to Providence, Rhode Island. From Providence, Davy went north by stagecoach to Boston, Massachusetts.

The land he looked out upon was completely unlike heavily forested western Tennessee. Davy called it "barren country."

He recalled that the Pilgrims had landed at Plymouth, not far from Boston. "It seems odd," he later wrote, "that they should have come all this way across the sea, and not look for good land."

Davy found the people of Boston to be kind and warmhearted. "When I arrived, I knew no one," he said, "but in a short time I made many acquaintances, and, indeed, was kindly treated by every person I met."

During his stay in Boston, Davy toured several mills and factories. In Tennessee, the only manufacturing plants turned out flour, lumber, paper, and gunpowder. Massachusetts, on the other hand, produced a tremendous variety of factory goods.

Davy went to a plant that made raincoats. He marveled at what he saw. "It was a great curiosity," he said, "to see young ladies cutting out the clothes, and sticking them together without sewing them. I also went through a shoe factory where they made shoes the same way, without stitching them."

Davy visited the town of Lowell, north of Boston. There factories with power looms turned out great quantities of wool and cotton cloth. "There are more than five thousand females employed in Lowell," Davy noted. "Some of the girls attended three looms, and they make from one dollar seventy-five cents to three dollars per week, after paying their board."

Davy was impressed with the efficiency. "Everything moves on like clock-work," he said.

Before leaving Boston, Davy was taken to the gold-domed State House. A statue of George

Washington that he saw there offended him. The general was wearing a military cloak. Davy mistakenly thought the cloak to be a Roman gown. "This ain't right," declared Davy. "He belonged to this country—heart, soul, and body, and I don't want any other to have any part of him—not even his clothes."

CHAPTER 10

DOUBLE DEFEAT

AFTER HIS THREE-WEEK TOUR OF THE Northeast, Davy returned home for the rest of the summer. He was back in Washington, D.C., when Congress met in the fall of 1834.

He continued to press for squatters' rights. He made little headway, though. His argument that the government ought to "at least occasionally legislate for the poor" fell on deaf ears.

Leaders of President Jackson's political party in the House of Representatives worried about Davy's land bill. If it became law, it would make Davy very popular in the West. They didn't want that. They blocked Davy's efforts at every turn.

In mid-February of the next year, 1835, Davy

was given a chance to speak for the land bill before Congress. But he was not able to get Congress to vote upon the measure.

Early in March, Congress closed down. Elections were to take place that summer. The members of Congress had to return home to campaign. They never voted on Davy's land bill.

In his three terms in Congress, Davy had not achieved very much. He had gone to Congress with one purpose in mind. He wanted to secure cheap land for the pioneer families of west Tennessee. He was not able to do that.

The land bill did not die, however. Several years later, Davy's son, John Wesley, continued his father's fight. John Wesley, like his father, became a member of Congress from Tennessee. He was elected in 1839 and again in 1841.

In 1841, John Wesley saw the land bill become law. Under its terms, federal land in Tennessee was to be given to the state. The state was then to sell the land for 12½ cents an acre. Those Tennesseans who lived on a particular piece of land were to be given a chance to buy it before anyone else.

Davy's ideas about public land were later taken up by the federal government. In 1862, President Abraham Lincoln signed the Homestead Act into law. It enabled any citizen to claim as much as 160 acres of public land. After living on a piece of land for five years, a settler could own it. The Homestead Act opened the West to millions of Americans.

As Davy began campaigning for reelection in 1835, he knew the race was going to be very close. President Andrew Jackson wanted to hear no more of the land bill. He wanted Davy defeated.

Jackson's forces picked another lawyer to run against Davy. His name was Adam Huntsman.

Davy's tour of the Northeast became an issue during the campaign. At the time Davy made the tour, Congress had been in session. There were votes to be made on important issues. Davy had not been there to cast his vote. Adam Huntsman made sure that people of west Tennessee knew that Davy had neglected his duty.

Nevertheless, Davy was convinced he was going to win the election. "If old Adam isn't beaten out of his hunting shirt, my name isn't Crockett," Davy said.

Davy was wrong. He was back home when the election results were brought to him. He lost by 230 votes.

Davy was deeply hurt by the defeat. He had already failed to get the land bill passed. Now he had lost his seat in Congress. In addition, the defeat had destroyed any hopes he might have had for running for president.

Davy felt proud about his service in Congress. He had fought for the land bill and the poor people of west Tennessee. He felt he had done the right thing. "I have done my duty..." he noted in his autobiography. "I have spoken the truth to the people of my district regardless of the consequences."

As for the future, Davy had exciting plans. He announced that he was going west to a place called Texas. At the time, Texas was part of Mexico. Even

After his election defeat in 1835, Davy said good-bye to politics, then began making preparations to go to Texas.

so, about 20,000 Americans lived there. They were anxious to break free of Mexico's rule.

Davy wasn't going to Mexico to join the fight for independence. To Davy, Texas was frontier country.

It was land to be explored. It was land to be tamed and settled.

His wife and children sobbed as Davy got ready to leave Tennessee. His plans were to return and get them later.

Finally the day of departure arrived. As Davy later recalled, "I started off . . . to take a steamboat down the Mississippi, and go ahead in a new world."

CHAPTER 11

ON TO TEXAS

DAVY DID NOT TRAVEL TO TEXAS alone. A nephew, William Patton, and a few friends went with him.

When the group arrived in Memphis, they and other friends enjoyed a farewell party. The next day they boarded a Mississippi River steamboat.

The steamboat carried them down the Mississippi to a point where it meets the Arkansas River. They boarded another steamboat, then traveled north on the Arkansas River to Little Rock. There a supper was held in Davy's honor.

From Little Rock, the group mounted horses and set out overland. They traveled south and west until they entered Red River country. Crossing the Red River, they entered Texas.

Heading south, they saw huge herds of buffalo and bands of wild horses. At night, great wildfires sometimes turned the sky orange. They reached Nacogdoches, Texas, on January 5, 1836.

Wherever he went, Davy discovered that people knew his name and folktales about him. "I am hailed with hearty welcome to this country," he wrote in a letter to his family. Upon his arrival in Nacogdoches, a cannon was fired in his honor.

Davy bubbled with enthusiasm for Texas. "It is the garden spot of the world," he said in a letter to his daughter Margaret and her husband. He described the area as having "the best land and best prospects for health I ever saw."

"I do believe," he continued, "it is a fortune to any man to come here."

In the letter, Davy also said that he had joined the army. "I have taken the oath of government," he said, "and have enrolled my name as a volunteer."

Oath of Allegiance Taken by Davy Crockett

I do solemnly swear that I will bear true allegiance to the Provisional Government of Texas or any future republican Government that may be hereafter declared, and that I will serve her honestly and faithfully against all her enemies and opposers whatsoever, and observe and obey the orders of the Governors of Texas, the orders and decrees of the present or future authorities and the orders of the officers appointed over me according to the rules and articles of the government of Texas, 'So help me God.'

Davy explained he had taken the oath in order to be able to vote. Elections would be held once Texas had won its independence. The oath taking would also allow Davy to run for public office.

Davy was truly excited by his future prospects. "I had rather be in my present situation than be elected to a seat in Congress for life," he told his daughter.

Davy's nephew, William Patton, also signed the

oath. Several others had joined their group by this time. They were called the Tennessee Mountain Volunteers.

There were about a dozen of them. Only half came from Tennessee. The rest were from Kentucky, Pennsylvania, and Ohio.

There were no professional soldiers in the group, which included two teenagers. Three of the men were lawyers. Two were doctors.

The volunteers had not come to Texas to be heroes in a war for independence. They simply wanted land.

Micajah Autry was one member of the group. He was, like Davy, a Tennessean who had little to show for a life of hard work. In a letter to his wife, Autry said, "Be of good cheer, Martha. I will provide you with a sweet home. I shall be entitled to 640 acres of land for my services in the army..."

The journey on horseback from Nacogdoches took about three weeks. Davy and his volunteers arrived on the outskirts of San Antonio on February 8, 1836.

Texas in 1836 was frontier country, a land to be explored, tamed, and settled.

At the time, San Antonio was a dusty settlement of small wood buildings. About 2,500 people lived there. Most of the residents were Mexican families.

Just east of the town, across the San Antonio River, stood an old mission. It was called the Alamo.

Spanish priests had founded the Alamo. They had moved out in 1793. Now Davy and the other rebels were turning the Alamo into a makeshift fortress.

The Alamo compound was of good size. It covered about four acres, an area a bit larger than a city block.

Thick walls of cut stone enclosed the compound. Within the walls were several buildings where soldiers lived. A mission church also stood on the property. Its walls were still upright but its roof had collapsed.

When Davy arrived in San Antonio, many people rushed to the town's central plaza to greet him. They had read the tall tales about Davy. They expected to see a man six-feet-four in his stocking feet, a man who could "whip his weight in wildcats."

The real Davy probably surprised them. He was forty-nine years old. He stood about five-feet-eight and was a bit thick waisted.

"I have come to your country, though not, I hope, through any selfish motive whatever," Davy told the crowd. "I have come to aid you all that I can in your noble cause . . ."

Two days later, a dance was held in Davy's honor. People danced all night long. They were still

Spanish priests built the Alamo's familiar mission church in 1757. They moved out in 1793.

dancing at around one o'clock in the morning when a scout came galloping into town. He brought scary news. The Mexican army was on the march, heading for San Antonio.

Antonio López de Santa Anna, the president of Mexico, led the army. His goal was to crush the rebel forces.

Colonel William B. Travis, the highest-ranking military officer at the Alamo, shrugged off the news. He had heard such reports before, he said. He had no faith in them. "Let us dance tonight," he proclaimed, "and make provisions for our defense tomorrow."

CHAPTER 12

SIEGE OF THE ALAMO

THE SCOUT'S REPORT WAS TRUE. Well-trained Mexican troops, numbering two to three thousand were on the march. They were heading north into Texas.

The huge well-prepared army stretched out for miles. First came the cavalry unit, men mounted on horses. Following them were long lines of soldiers on foot. The army's supply train was next. It was made up of hundreds of horse-drawn carts and wagons. A thousand pack mules followed. They carried food, weapons, and ammunition. The Mexican army was ready for a long fight.

Sam Houston, commander in chief of the Texas military forces, was worried. He did not want his small ragtag army to meet the Mexicans in a face-to-face battle. That would be certain defeat. The rebels would be quickly overpowered by the mass of Mexican soldiers.

About three weeks before Davy and his volunteers arrived in San Antonio, Houston had sent Colonel James Bowie to the Alamo. Bowie was a trusted friend of Houston's. He carried orders to abandon the Alamo and then blow it up.

Colonel James Clinton Neill, the commander of the Alamo at the time, welcomed Bowie. The two colonels discussed Houston's plan. They decided that destroying the Alamo would be a mistake. The Alamo must be defended, they believed. They agreed to ignore Sam Houston's orders.

Meanwhile, the Mexican army moved steadily toward Texas. By February 21, the Mexican troops had reached the Medina River. San Antonio was only twenty-five miles to the north.

Before dawn on February 23, Colonel Travis was awakened by the sound of oxcarts moving out of town. San Antonio was emptying out. The residents were loading the contents of their homes into carts and leaving.

Travis soon learned why. A messenger had arrived during the night. He brought word from the Mexican army. All Mexican civilians were to leave San Antonio. Santa Anna planned to attack the next day.

Americans in San Antonio fled to the Alamo. The gates to the compound were closed and barred. Inside were about 150 fighting men. Thirty to forty civilians were there, too.

Davy did not like the situation. He felt trapped. "I think we had better march out and die in the open air," he said. "I don't like being hemmed up."

During the afternoon, the Mexican cavalry rode into San Antonio. The foot soldiers quickly followed. Santa Anna's forces occupied the town without firing a shot.

With San Antonio in their control, the Mexicans turned their attention to the Alamo. They moved their artillery into position and began firing at the fort. Cannonballs tore into roofs and walls.

At the time Davy Crockett and his volunteers arrived at the Alamo, William B. Travis was the highest-ranking military officer at the fortress.

Santa Anna's troops began to surround the Alamo. They were careful to stay at least 200 yards away from the outside walls. That was the range of the Kentucky long rifles with which Davy and some of the other rebels were armed.

Davy and his Tennessee Mountain Volunteers were assigned a position by the battered church. It was a weak point in the Alamo defenses. Travis knew it would be stronger with Davy and his volunteers behind it.

Like the other rebels, Davy and his men could

Some of the Alamo defenders dressed in buckskins and armed themselves with Kentucky long rifles.

only watch and wait. When there was a lull in the deafening artillery fire, they ate and slept.

A survivor of the siege later recalled Davy's talent with a fiddle. At times when the Mexican guns were silent, Davy would play a few tunes. This helped the men to relax.

Sometimes there was bagpipe music, too. From time to time Davy and the bagpiper, John McGregor, would play together. The music rising from behind the Alamo's walls must have sounded odd to the Mexican soldiers outside.

Occasionally the rebels loaded one of their cannons and fired toward the Mexican troops. Their cannon powder and shot were in short supply, though. They thought they should save their ammunition.

Mexican artillerymen kept moving their cannons closer and closer. The bombardment continued with hardly any letup. Day by day, hour by hour, more Mexican soldiers arrived.

Before dawn on the morning of March 6, the men within the Alamo heard the blaring of Mexican bugles. It was a signal that an attack was coming. The sound of the bugles died. Then hundreds upon hundreds of Mexican soldiers streamed toward the Alamo's walls.

Davy's sharpshooters turned back the Mexicans that were attacking the south wall. On the north side, a handful of Mexicans managed to reach the wall. Colonel Travis was posted there. He looked down and fired his shotgun at the Mexican soldiers clustered below.

Suddenly Travis went down. He had taken a bullet in the forehead. Travis was one of the first defenders killed at the Alamo.

The rebels managed to slow the Mexican attack.

March 6, 1836: The Mexican army launches its final assault upon the Alamo.

But the pause was only a short one. Mexican officers ordered their men forward a second time. Heavy fire from the rebels turned back that assault, too.

The Mexicans came a third time. A swarm of soldiers reached the north wall. Bare timbers supported a damaged section of the wall. Some of the soldiers scrambled up the timbers and over the wall. Once inside, they opened a gate. Dozens of attackers poured through it.

At about the same time, another swarm of

attacking troops charged the northwest wall. Several holes had been punched in the wall by cannons. Soldiers squeezed through the holes. They opened another gate. More Mexican soldiers rushed in. At the southeast corner of the compound, troops scaled the wall with ladders.

Savage hand-to-hand fighting followed. The rebels fought using knives and bayonets. Some wielded their rifles like clubs.

The struggle did not last long. The Mexicans quickly overwhelmed the rebels.

Santa Anna had given an order that only women were to be spared. That order was carried out. Mexican troops killed every soldier they could find.

CHAPTER 13

FINAL MOMENTS

DURING THE HEAT OF THE ALAMO struggle, Davy fought bravely. A letter from an Alamo defender said, "Davy Crockett and James Bowy [Bowie] are fighting at San Antone [Antonio] like Tigers."

A letter written from San Augustine, Texas, on March 29, stated: "The Honorable David Crockett . . . was found dead with about twenty of the enemy with him and his rifle broken to pieces. [It] is supposed that he killed at least twenty to thirty himself."

In the final stages of the battle, Davy was thought to have fought fiercely. After he ran out of ammunition, he was said to have swung Old Betsey by the barrel, clubbing the attackers.

Several women survived the massacre. Señora Candelaria was believed to have been one of them. She recalled Davy's last moments. "Davy Crockett died fighting like a wild beast within a few feet of me," she said. "[He] was killed near the entrance to the church, his rifle in his hands. He was the last to die."

Historians now question Señora Candelaria's statements. Other accounts of Davy's death are believed to be more accurate. One is based on a diary kept by one of Santa Anna's officers. It was first published in English in 1975.

According to the diary, Mexican troops went on a room-to-room search after the fighting stopped. They were looking for anyone who might have remained alive. They found half a dozen survivors. They were hiding in a dark back room. One was Davy Crockett.

Some of the troops wanted to slaughter the men they had found. "No!" said General Manuel Fernandez Castrillón, raising a hand. The general did not want any more killing.

General Castrillón led the Americans across the Alamo plaza to where Santa Anna was standing.

"Santa Anna," said Castrillón, "I deliver to you six brave prisoners of war."

Santa Anna scowled at his general. His instructions had been that no prisoners were to be taken. "I do not want to see these men living," Santa Anna declared. "Shoot them!"

The diary states, "The commanders and officers were outraged at this action and did not support the order. But several officers who were around the president . . . thrust themselves forward." These men, "with swords in hand, fell upon these unfortunate defenseless men just as a tiger leaps upon its prey."

Davy and the others "died without complaining and without humiliating themselves," says the diary.

Several Mexican soldiers witnessed what took place. They declared the diary account of Davy Crockett's final moments to be true.

News of the Alamo battle and the terrible slaughter there enraged Texans. "Remember the Alamo!" became their battle cry.

The remains of Davy Crockett, William B. Travis, Jim Bowie, and other Alamo defenders are sealed in a marble casket in San Antonio's San Fernando Cathedral.

At San Jacinto, Texas, on April 21, 1836, a rebel force under the command of Sam Houston caught Santa Anna's army by surprise. In the battle that followed, the rebels scored a major victory, driving the Mexican army out of Texas.

Sam Houston had been the governor of Tennessee before moving to Texas.

Earlier, Texas had declared its independence from Mexico. After the battle of San Jacinto, the settlers made Houston president of the Republic of Texas.

The massacre at the Alamo and the news of Davy's death deeply saddened the people of Tennessee. In Nashville, men and women were seen to weep openly.

Of Davy, one observer wrote, "None ever knew him personally who did not love him. None who were familiar with his public career that did not admire him.

"The whole people of the state were then, as now, proud of him."

CHAPTER 14

A LEGEND SPROUTS

The people of Tennessee had a right to be proud of Davy Crockett. He was a good man. He was a colorful frontiersman. He was an outstanding hunter and a brave soldier. As a member of Congress, he tried to help poor families of west Tennessee. He fought heroically at the Alamo.

These are worthy achievements. They may or may not have been enough to earn Davy Crockett lasting fame.

Nevertheless, in the years after his death, Davy Crockett's legend spread. By the mid-1800s, Davy Crockett had become, like Pocahontas or Paul Revere, a great American folk hero.

Towns in Texas and California adopted his name. Counties in Texas and Tennessee were named in his honor. Songs and plays were written about him. Steamboats, parks, and schools took Davy Crockett's name.

The Crockett almanacs helped to give Davy Crockett legendary fame. The almanacs were small books that were published between 1835 and 1856. There were about fifty different titles.

They are believed to have been printed in New York, Philadelphia, Boston, Baltimore, and Nashville. They were popular everywhere.

Like any almanac, each of these contained a calendar for each month of the coming year. It gave the time of sunrises and sunsets.

But the Crockett almanacs contained much more. They were filled with cartoony drawings and larger-than-life adventure tales. In these, Davy was presented as a frontier superhero.

In one of the almanacs, Davy boasted that he could run faster, jump higher, squat lower, dive deeper—and come out drier—than anyone else.

Cartoonlike drawings were featured throughout the almanacs. Here Davy narrowly escapes a huge snake.

"I've got the fastest horse, surest rifle, prettiest sister, and ugliest dog in the state of Tennessee," he said.

In another of the tall tales, Davy tells of standing under a tree during a fierce thunderstorm. For some time, he dodged the lightning bolts. He got bored with that, though. He then sprawled out and took a series of electric jolts. These did Davy no harm. They merely hardened his head and "made him ready for all comers."

Even Davy's snoring had a super quality to it. It was said that he snored so loudly that he had to sleep in a house across the street. Otherwise, he would wake himself up.

In a story titled "The Boat Race," Davy wins by using a wildcat as an outboard motor.

Other people in the almanacs also had super qualities. One of Davy's uncles shaved himself with sheet lightning. On hot days, he fanned himself with a hurricane. He ate pickled thunderbolts for breakfast. He could drink the Mississippi dry.

Davy is named as the author of the almanacs. Most historians agree, however, that he had

One of Davy's uncles was said to have incredible qualities: He picked his teeth with a pitchfork and combed his hair with a rake.

nothing to do with them. No one knows who wrote them.

In one of the stories, Davy displays his cleverness and quick wit. His wife was once being taken advantage of by a Yankee horse trader. She had agreed to pay forty dollars for a horse that was worthless. "The hoss [horse]," Davy said, "was lame in his forelegs and hind legs, too. He was blind of one eye and deaf of both ears."

When the dealer came to the Crockett home to collect his money, Davy was ready for him. He had put an old saddle and bridle on the horse.

Davy had gone into the woods and found a hornet's nest. He plugged the top of the nest so the hornets couldn't get out. He brought the nest back home with him.

When the dealer arrived to collect his money, Davy greeted him with a smile. He praised the horse. There was one problem, he said. The animal was so spirited that his wife couldn't ride him.

He asked the dealer to get on the horse to "see how it would go." Once the dealer was in the saddle,

Davy plotted to get even with "the Yankee horse jockey" who tried to take advantage of his wife.

Davy grabbed the hornet's nest and pulled out the plug. He then "flung it agin [against] the hoss's backsides."

"The animal showed some spirit then," Davy reported, "for the little varmints cum [came] out [and] he set out on full run...

"The hoss then dug through the forest, without stopping to count the leaves," Davy said. As for the poor dealer, he "clung to the hoss's mane like a chesnut [chestnut] burr to bearskin.

"The last I heered [heard] of him, he was seen up

by the fork of Duck River, going through the country like a runaway steamboat."

The story had a happy ending. "He [the dealer] never cum [came] back arter [after] his money." Davy noted.

Even though many stories in the almanacs were fantasy, they were important. They helped to assure that the story of Davy Crockett did not end with his death. In fact, they triggered even greater fame for the Tennessee-born frontiersman.

CHAPTER 15

DAVY CROCKETT REMEMBERED

THE STORY OF DAVY CROCKETT GOES well beyond his actual lifetime. After his death, the almanacs helped Davy to become a legendary hero in American history.

No one then could have imagined what would happen next. During the mid-1950s, the nation was swept by a great Davy Crockett craze.

A television series based on Davy's life touched off the mania. The series had three one-hour episodes. The first made its debut in December 1954. The next two appeared early in 1955.

By the spring of 1955, the Davy Crockett craze was in full swing. Older children were

Fess Parker (left) starred as television's Davy Crockett during the 1950s.

caught up in it first. Then younger children discovered it.

Store shelves were crammed with many hundreds of different Davy Crockett toys and other items. There were Davy Crockett lunch boxes, toy telephones, bath towels, wallets, and toothbrushes. There were puzzles and board games. There were comic books and trading cards.

Kids loved wearing Davy Crockett clothing. Boys and girls wore fringed leather jackets and pants and pajamas and underwear. Department stores set up special sections to sell the clothing.

The coonskin cap became a symbol for the craze. Every child from two to twelve wanted to own one. Some kids insisted on wearing their caps to bed. Millions were sold.

"The Ballad of Davy Crockett" became the nation's number one song. It had eighteen verses. More than four million records of the song were sold.

At the height of the craze, schoolteachers claimed that they couldn't teach. Their students

During the Davy Crockett craze of the mid-1950s, three of his descendants posed for this picture.

were paying too much attention to Davy Crockett. They said, "kids need to be calmed down."

The Davy Crockett craze faded fast. By the end of 1955, it was over.

Hollywood turned to Davy Crockett's story again in 1960. That's when the movie *The Alamo* was

Hollywood superstar John Wayne (center) played the role of Davy Crockett in The Alamo, *a feature film released in 1960.*

released. The film starred John Wayne as Davy Crockett.

Wayne was a Hollywood superstar at the time. He was famous for playing cowboys and war heroes. He had starred in films like *Stagecoach* and *Operation Pacific*.

John Wayne portrayed Davy as intelligent and honest with a good sense of humor. Davy was a gallant hero in the movie.

John Wayne did not look like the real Davy Crockett. Wayne was tall, about six-feet-four. He had a slim figure. He looked like the fictional folk hero described in the Crockett almanacs.

At the time of the battle of the Alamo in 1836, the real Davy Crockett was stocky and of about average height. But it is likely that the image of Davy as created by John Wayne is the one that remains in the public's mind.

There are many reminders of Davy Crockett at the Alamo in San Antonio. Nearly three million people visit the Alamo each year.

Davy's buckskin vest is on display inside the old mission church. Paving stones in the Alamo Plaza indicate the section of the fortress defended by Davy and the Tennessee volunteers.

A sculpted image of Davy is part of a striking marble monument that rises from the edge of Alamo Plaza. It honors the men who died there. Davy, standing next to Travis, wears his fringed hunting jacket. His rifle is at his side.

The memory of Davy Crockett lives on. Thanks to the Crockett almanacs, Davy became an American folk hero. Through movies and television, Davy has been introduced to new generations. The legend of Davy Crockett keeps growing.

CHRONOLOGY

1786	(August 17) Davy Crockett is born in Limestone, Tennessee.
1806	Marries Mary (Polly) Finley.
1811	Family moves to Lincoln County, Tennessee.
1813	Family moves to Franklin County, Tennessee.
1813	Enlists in the militia in Winchester, Tennessee.
1815	Wife Polly dies.
1816	Marries Elizabeth Patton.
1817	Crocketts settle in Lawrence County, Tennessee.
1821–24	Serves in Tennessee state legislature.
1822	Crocketts settle near Obion River in west Tennessee.
1827	Elected to Congress.
1829	Reelected to Congress.
1831	Defeated in Congressional election.
1833	Reelected to Congress.
1834	Tours major cities of the Northeast.
1835	Defeated in Congressional election.
1836	Signs oath of allegiance to provisional government of Texas.
1836	(March 6) Dies at the Alamo.

BIBLIOGRAPHY

Primary Sources

Meine, Franklin J., ed. *The Crockett Almanacs, Nashville Series, 1835–1838*. Chicago: The Caxton Club, 1955.

Folmsbee, Stanley J. and James A. Shackford, eds. *David Crockett, A Narrative of the Life of David Crockett of the State of Tennessee*. Knoxville: University of Tennessee Press, 1973.

Lofaro, Michael A., ed. *Davy Crockett, The Man, The Legend, The Legacy, 1786–1986*. Knoxville: University of Tennessee Press, 1985.

The Tall Tales of Davy Crockett, The Second Nashville Series of Crockett Almanacs, 1839–1841. Knoxville: University of Tennessee Press, 1987.

Secondary Sources

Anderson, Paul. *The Davy Crockett Craze*. Hillside, IL: R & G Productions, 1996.

Cummings, Joe and Michael A. Lofaro, eds. *Crockett at Two Hundred: New Perspectives on the Man and the Myth*. Knoxville: University of Tennessee Press, 1989.

Derr, Mark. *The Frontiersman: The Real Life and Many Legends of Davy Crockett*. New York: William Morrow, 1993.

Kilgore, Dan. *How Did Davy Die?* College Station: Texas Press A&M University Press, 1978.

Long, Jeff. *Duel of Eagles: The Mexican and U.S. Fight for the Alamo*. New York: William Morrow, 1990.

Rourke, Constance. *Davy Crockett*. Lincoln: University of Nebraska Press, 1998.

FURTHER READING

Adler, David A. *A Picture Book of Davy Crockett*. New York: Holiday House, 1998.

Chermerka, William D. *The Davy Crockett Almanac and Book of Lists*. Austin, TX: Eakin Publications, 2000.

Fisher, Leonard Everett. *The Alamo*. New York: Holiday House, 1987.

Hauch, Richard Boyd. *Davy Crockett: A Handbook*. Lincoln: University of Nebraska Press, 1986.

Mosely, Elizabeth R. *Davy Crockett, Hero of the Wild Frontier*. New York: Chelsea House, 1991.

FOR MORE INFORMATION

Davy Crockett Birthplace

Request a brochure describing the Davy Crockett birthplace site and state park:

State of Tennessee
Department of Environment and Conservation
Davy Crockett Birthplace
1245 Davy Crockett Park Road
Limestone, TN 37681
Phone: (423) 257-2167

Davy Crockett Spring and Campsite

Request information describing historical features of Crockett, Texas:

Historical Commission
Houston County Courthouse
Crockett, TX 75835
Phone (936) 544-3255, Ext. 238

The Alamo

Request brochure "The Story of the Alamo," published by the Daughters of the Republic of Texas:

The Alamo
P. O. Box 2599
San Antonio, TX 78299
Phone: (210) 225-1391
Fax: (210) 229-1343

Web site: www.TheAlamo.org

Note: For a state-by-state (or province-by-province) listing of libraries, colleges, historical societies, and other institutions where primary sources are to be found, visit this Web site:

www.uidaho.edu/special-collections/east2.html

ACKNOWLEDGMENTS

Many people helped me in providing background information, photographs and other artwork for use in this book. Special thanks are due Hilda Pruitt, Davy Crockett Birthplace, Limestone, Tennessee; Eliza Bishop, Houston County (Texas) Historical Commission; Bill Grubbs, Cleburne (Texas) State Park; Jane Karotkyn, Friends of the Governor's Mansion, Austin, Texas; Diane Black and Karina McDonald, Tennessee State Library and Archives; Maja Keech, Prints and Photographs Division, Library of Congress; Heather Egan, National Portrait Gallery; Leslie Hirsch, the University of Texas at Austin; Cathy Herpich, Texas History Research Library at the Alamo; Tom Shelton, the University of Texas Institute of Texas Cultures, San Antonio; Sal Alberti and James Lowe, James Lowe Autographs, and Bill Sullivan.

George Sullivan, New York City

PHOTO CREDITS

National Portrait Gallery: 7, 25, 71; Library of Congress: 10, 33, 55, 98, 111; Tennessee State Library and Archives: 15; Davy Crockett Birthplace, Limestone, TN: 18; New York Public Library: 38, 41, 45, 47, 49, 73, 82, 108, 109; R.M. Smythe & Co.: 63; New York Museum of Natural History: 66; Texas State Library, Archives Division: 88, 95; The Daughters of the Republic of Texas Library: 90; Danal Terry: 96; George Sullivan: 103; Associated Press/Wide World Photos: 104, 116; Movie Star News: 114, 117

INDEX

Bold numbers refer to photographs

ABOUT THE AUTHOR

George Sullivan is the author of a good-sized shelf of books for children and young adults. They cover a wide range of topics, from witchcraft to nuclear submarines; from baseball and field hockey to photography.

His interest in photography goes beyond just writing about it. He often takes photos to illustrate his books.

His other titles for Scholastic include *Mr. President: Facts and Fun About the Presidents*, *100 Years in Photographs*, and *Alamo!*

For the In Their Own Words series, he has written biographies of Paul Revere, Lewis and Clark, Abraham Lincoln, Helen Keller, Harriet Tubman, and Pocahontas.

Mr. Sullivan was born in Lowell, Massachusetts, and brought up in Springfield, where he attended public school.

Mr. Sullivan graduated from Fordham University and worked in public relations in New York City before turning to writing on a full-time basis.

He lives in New York City with his wife. He is a member of PEN, the American Society of Journalists and Authors, and the Authors Guild.